Piano Duets

Movie Hits for Two

Arranged by Ann Collins

Artwork © The Walt Disney Company

ISBN 0-7935-3922-6

7777 W. BLUEMOUND RD. P.O. BOX 13819 MILWAUKEE, WI 53213

THE BARE NECESSITIES

from Walt Disney's THE JUNGLE BOOK

Words and Music by
TERRY GILKYSON

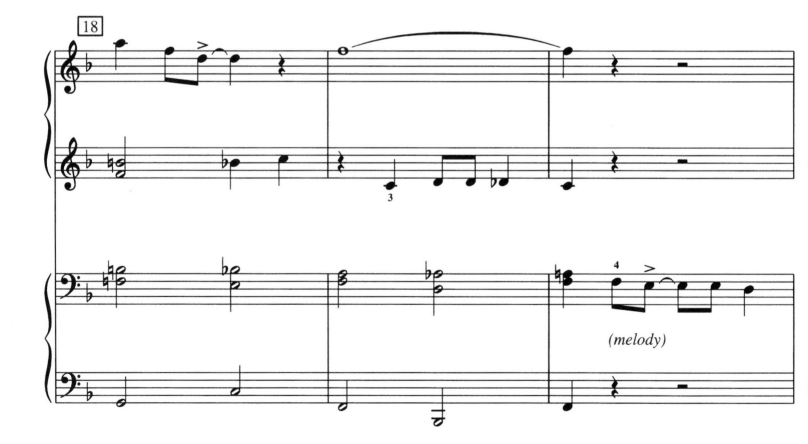

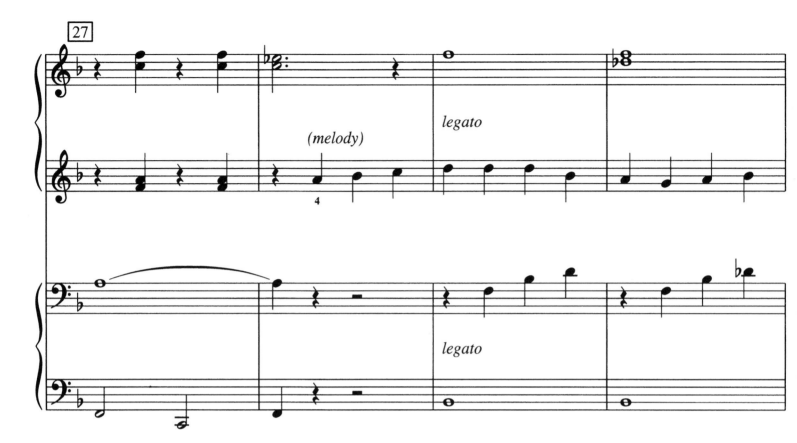

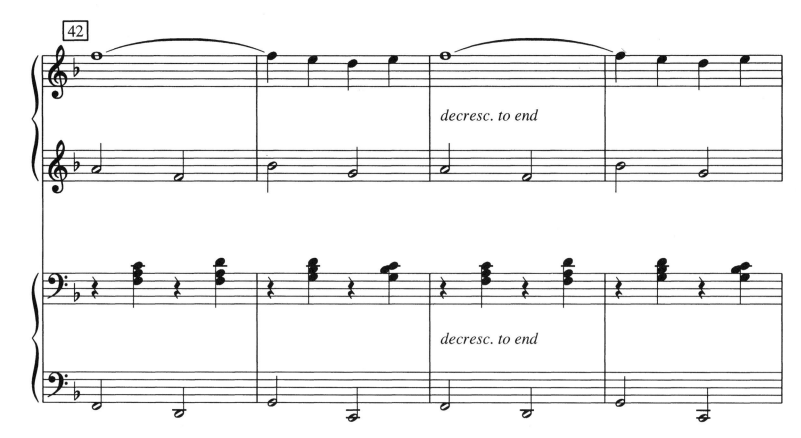

decresc. to end

decresc. to end

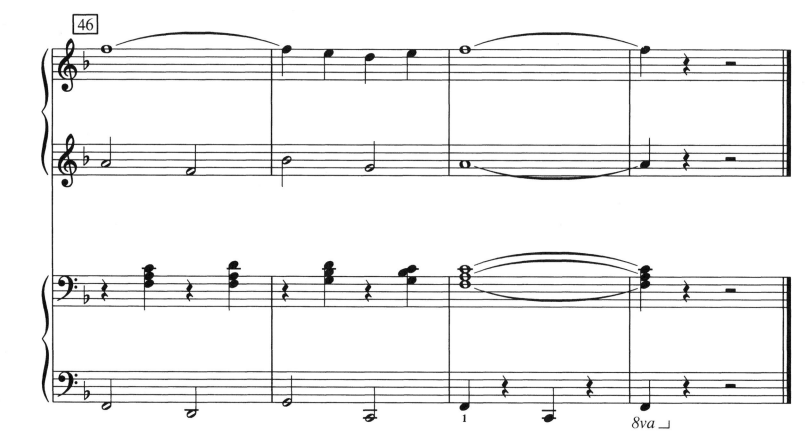

BE OUR GUEST

from Walt Disney's BEAUTY AND THE BEAST

Lyrics by HOWARD ASHMAN
Music by ALAN MENKEN

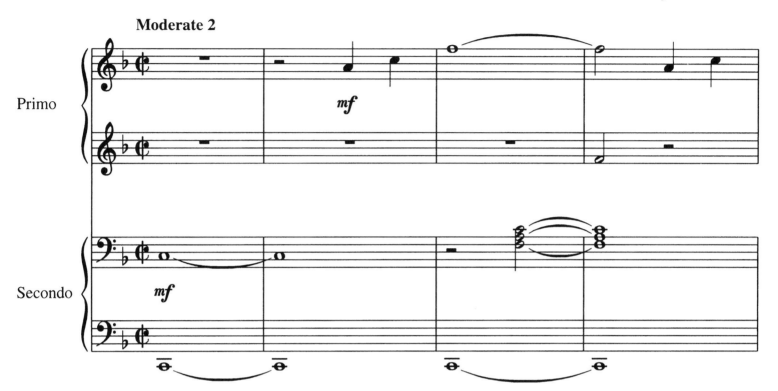

Brightly

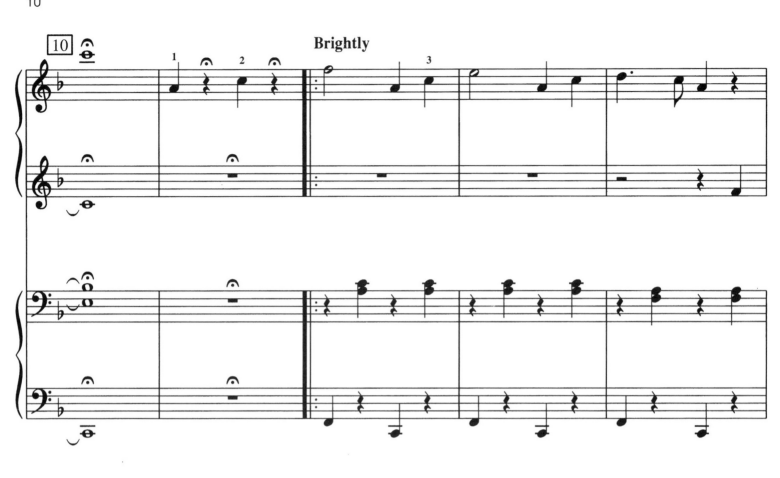

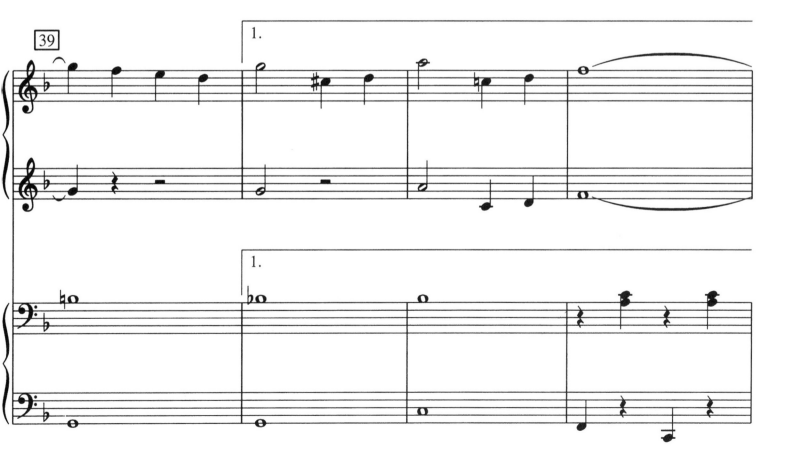

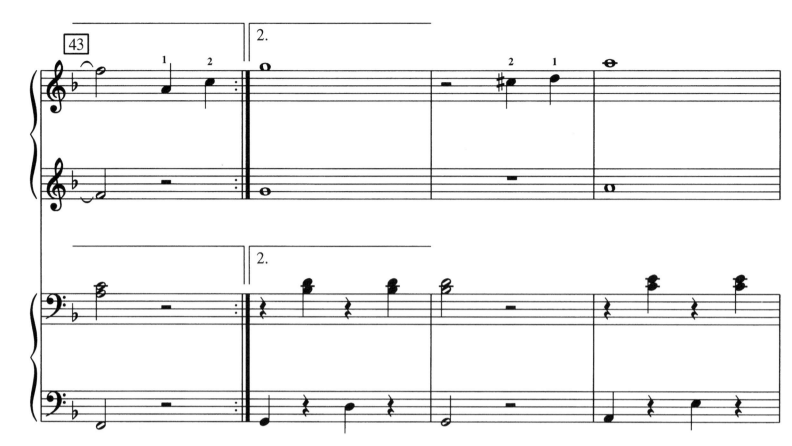

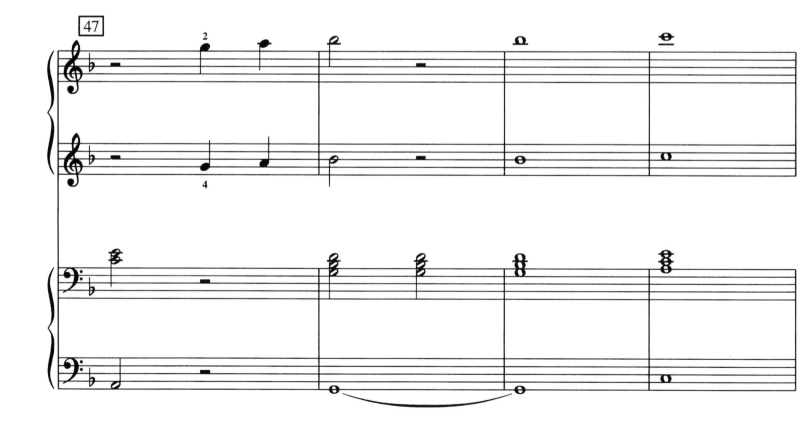

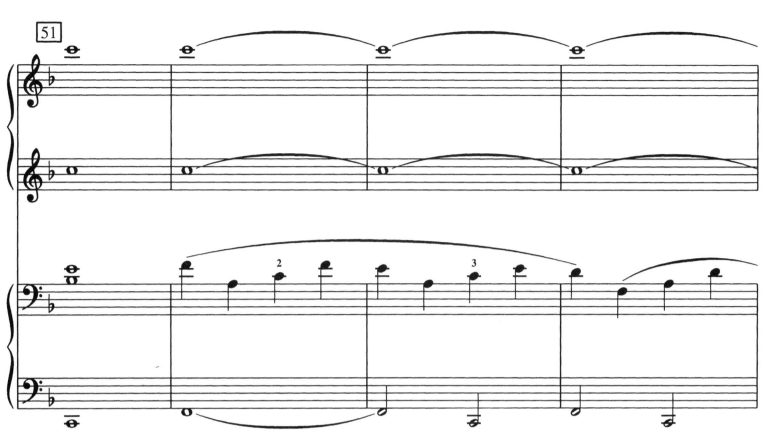

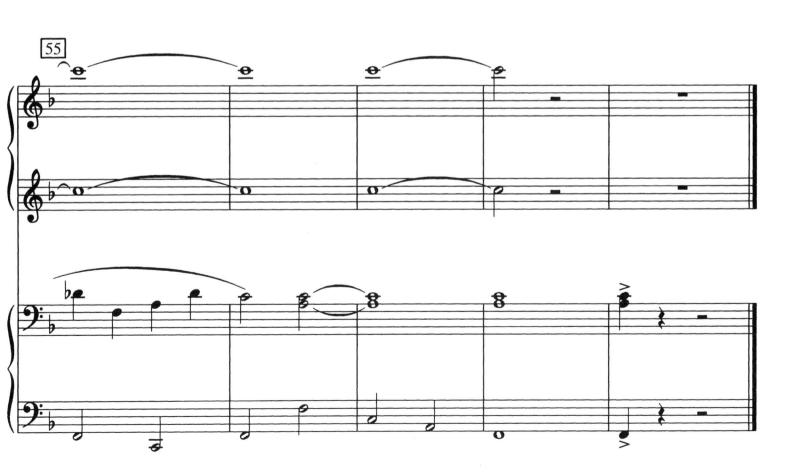

BEAUTY AND THE BEAST

from Walt Disney's BEAUTY AND THE BEAST

Lyrics by HOWARD ASHMAN
Music by ALAN MENKEN

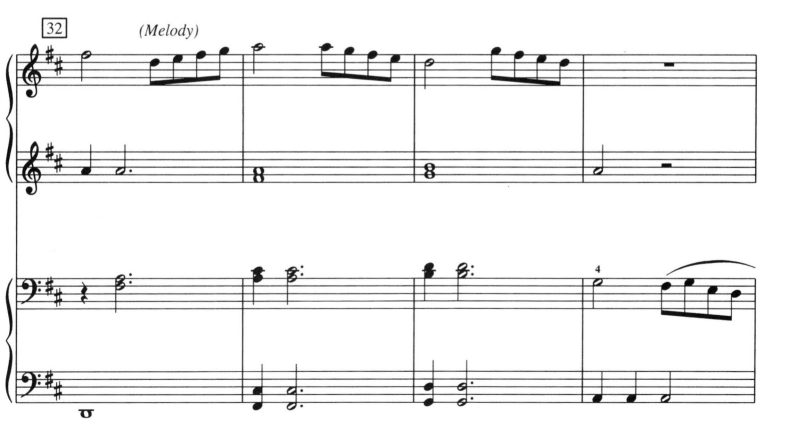

CIRCLE OF LIFE

from Walt Disney Pictures' THE LION KING

Music by ELTON JOHN
Lyrics by TIM RICE

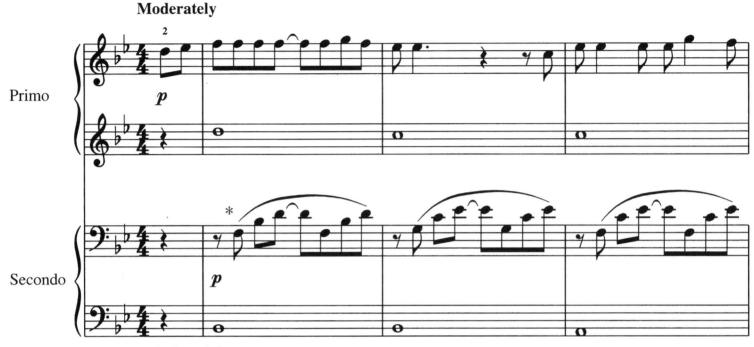

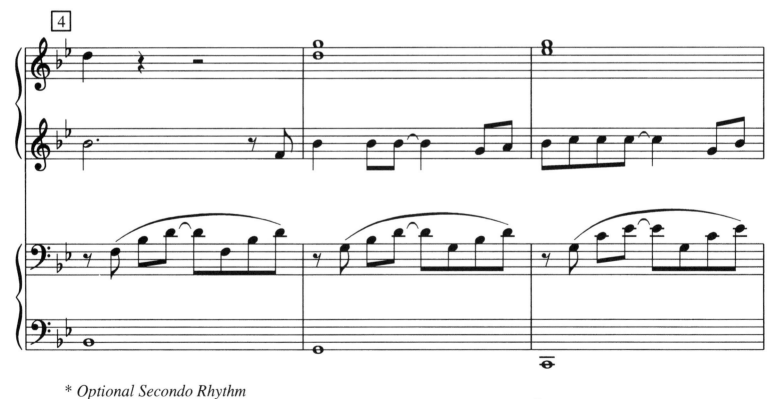

Optional Secondo Rhythm

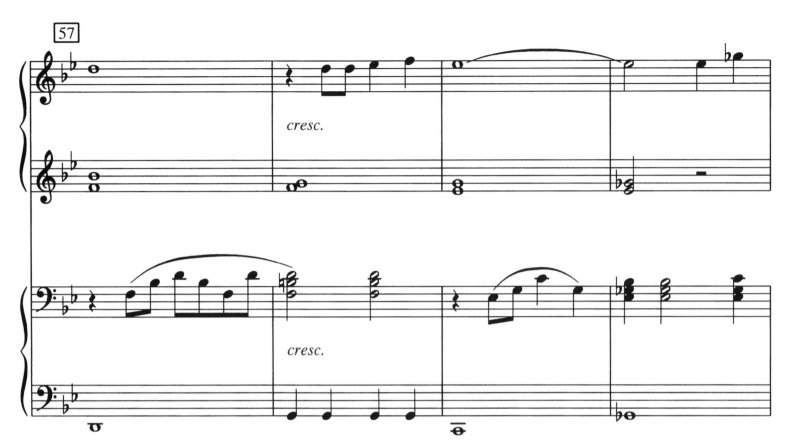

8vb

UNDER THE SEA
from Walt Disney's THE LITTLE MERMAID

Lyrics by HOWARD ASHMAN
Music by ALAN MENKEN

FRIEND LIKE ME
from Walt Disney's ALADDIN

Lyrics by HOWARD ASHMAN
Music by ALAN MENKEN

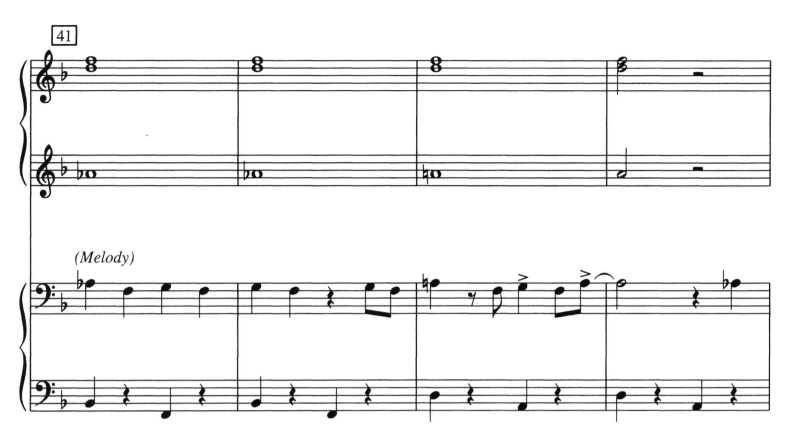

I JUST CAN'T WAIT TO BE KING

from Walt Disney Pictures' THE LION KING

Music by ELTON JOHN
Lyrics by TIM RICE

D.C. al Fine

PART OF YOUR WORLD

from Walt Disney's THE LITTLE MERMAID

Lyrics by HOWARD ASHMAN
Music by ALAN MENKEN

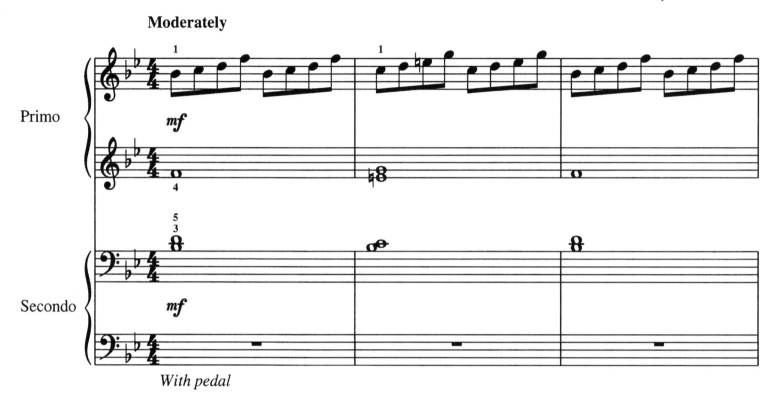

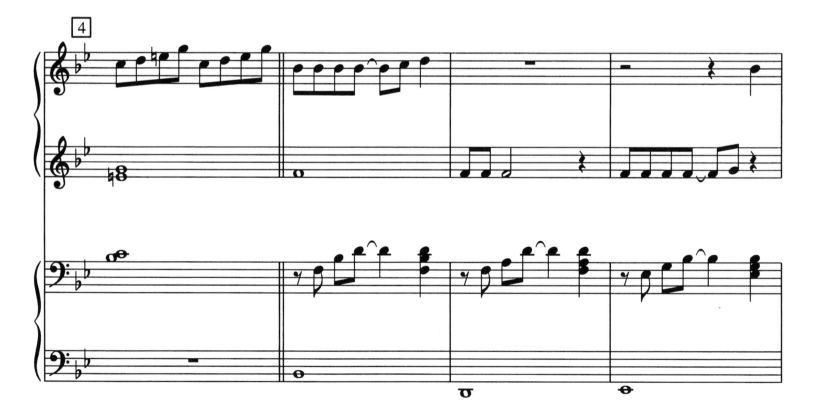

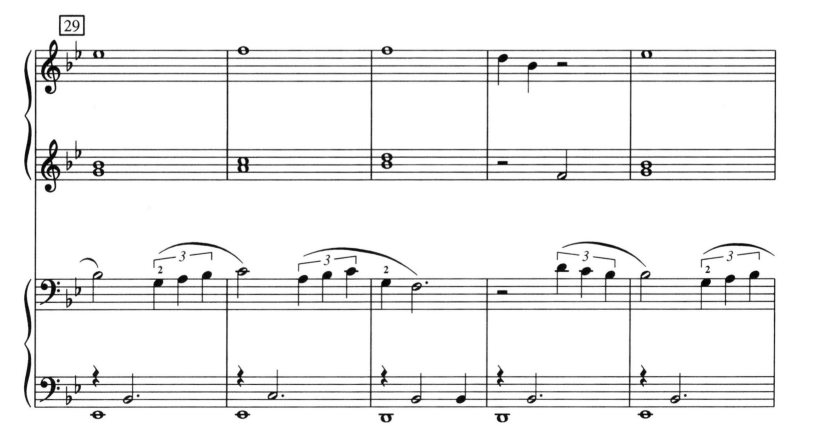

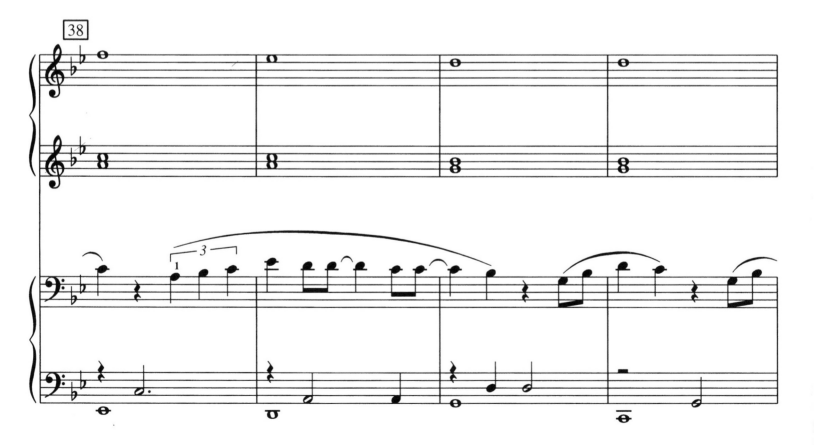

(Melody)

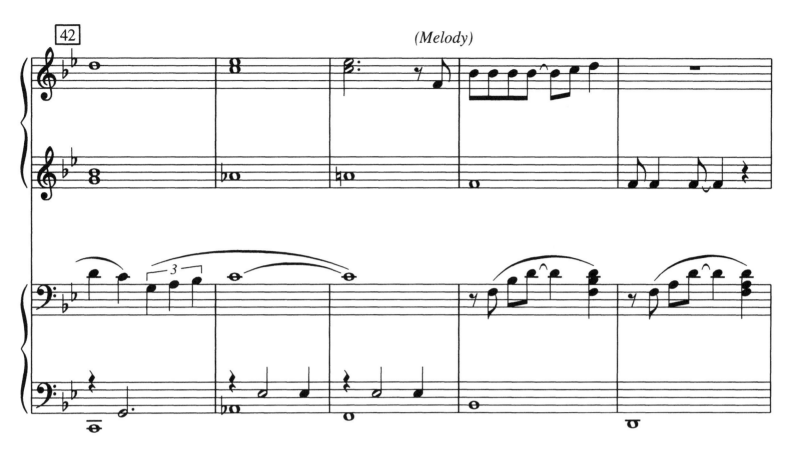

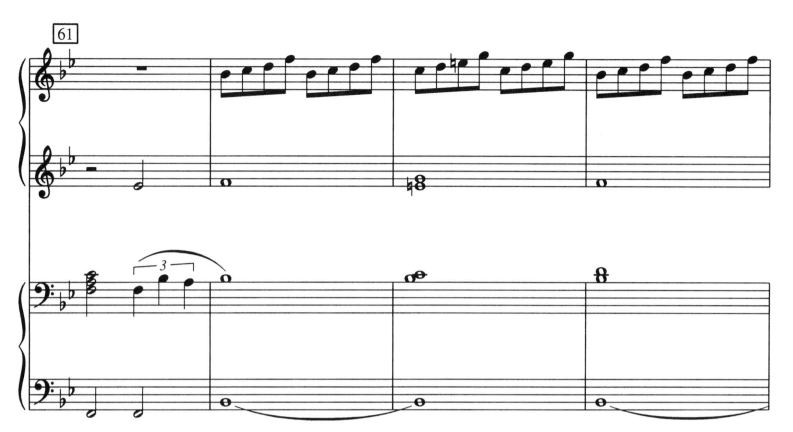

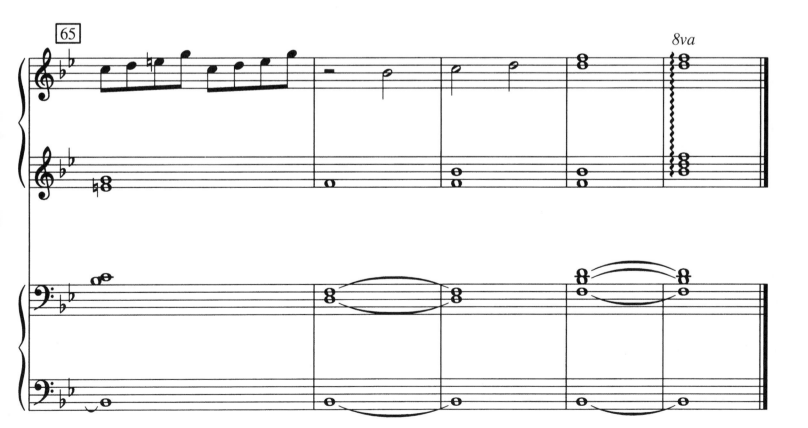

A WHOLE NEW WORLD

from Walt Disney's ALADDIN

Music by ALAN MENKEN
Lyrics by TIM RICE

Moderately, with expression

Primo

Secondo

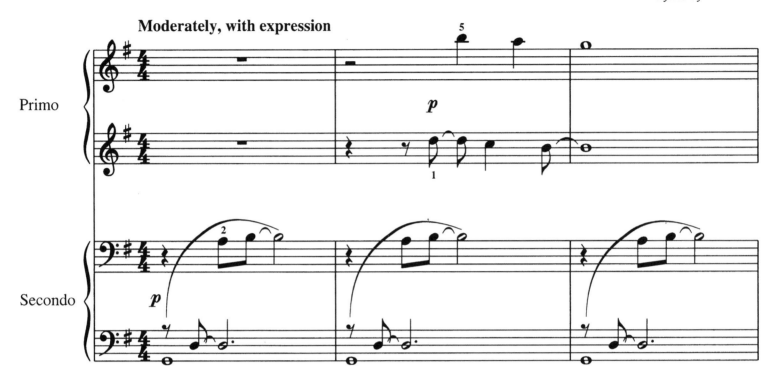

Both hands one octave higher 2nd time

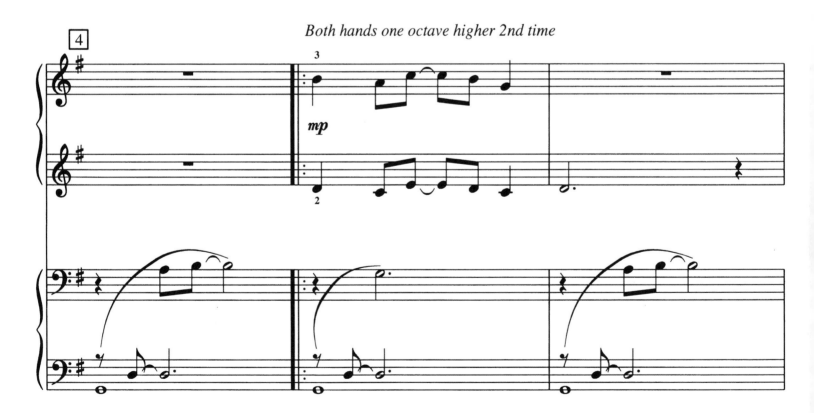

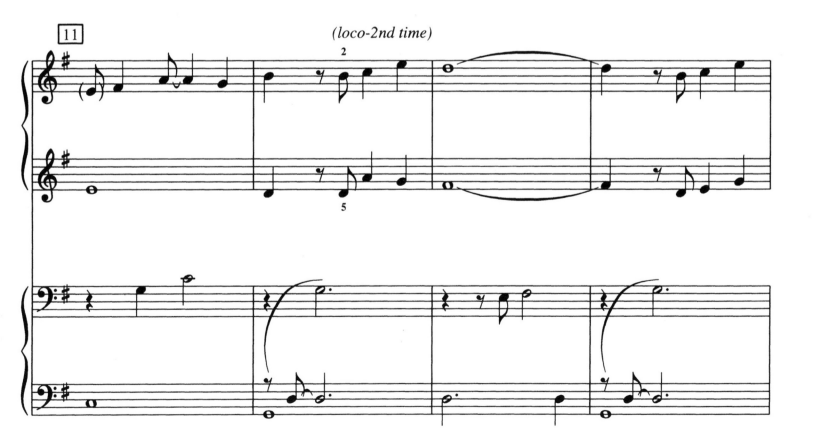

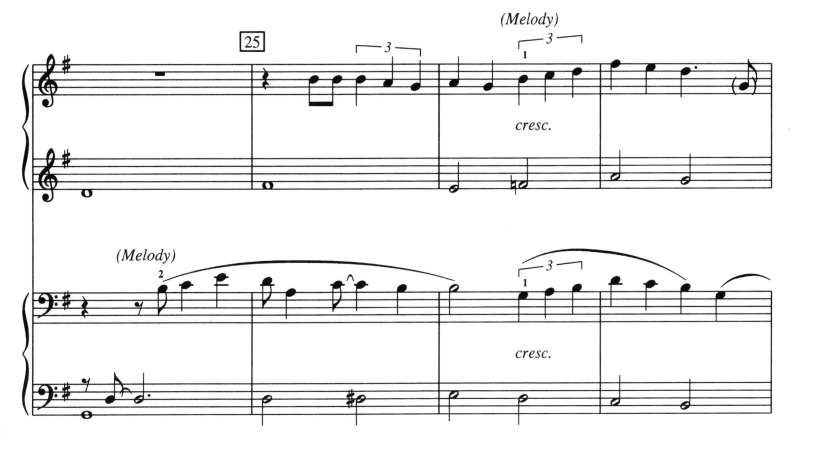

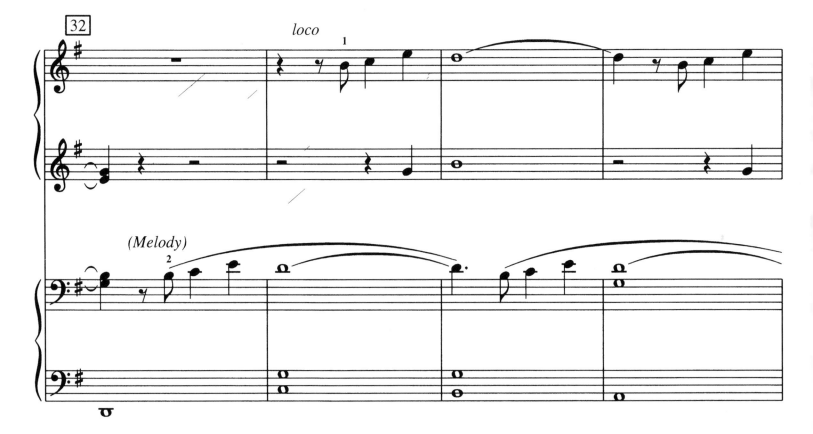

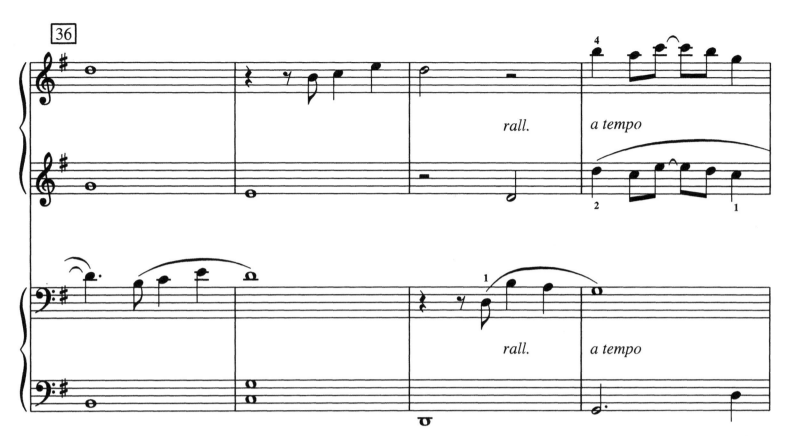

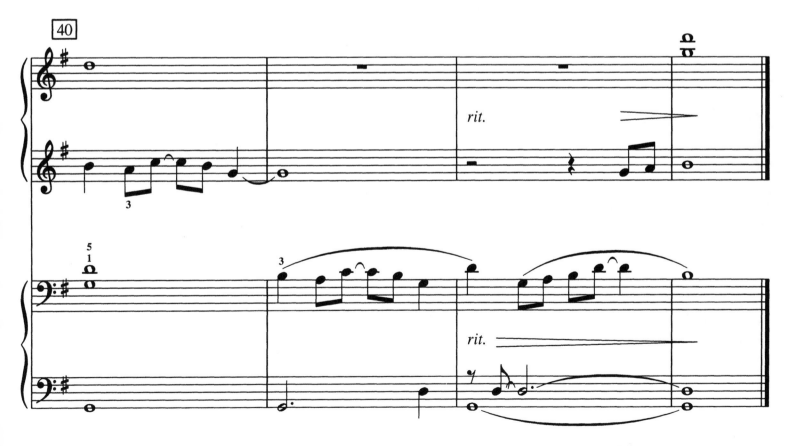

Piano for Two

A VARIETY OF PIANO DUETS FROM HAL LEONARD

ADELE FOR PIANO DUET

Eight of Adele's biggest hits arranged especially for intermediate piano duet! Featuring: Chasing Pavements • Hello • Make You Feel My Love • Rolling in the Deep • Set Fire to the Rain • Skyfall • Someone Like You • When We Were Young.

00172162..................... $14.99

CONTEMPORARY DISNEY DUETS

8 Disney piano duets to play and perform with a friend! Includes: Almost There • He's a Pirate • I See the Light • Let It Go • Married Life • That's How You Know • Touch the Sky • We Belong Together.

00128259 .... $12.99

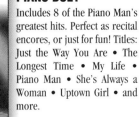

BILLY JOEL FOR PIANO DUET

Includes 8 of the Piano Man's greatest hits. Perfect as recital encores, or just for fun! Titles: Just the Way You Are • The Longest Time • My Life • Piano Man • She's Always a Woman • Uptown Girl • and more.

00141139 .... $14.99

THE BEATLES PIANO DUETS – 2ND EDITION

Features 8 arrangements: Can't Buy Me Love • Eleanor Rigby • Hey Jude • Let It Be • Penny Lane • Something • When I'm Sixty-Four • Yesterday.

00290496..................... $15.99

EASY CLASSICAL DUETS

7 great piano duets to perform at a recital, play-for-fun, or sightread! Titles: By the Beautiful Blue Danube (Strauss) • Eine kleine Nachtmusik (Mozart) • Sleeping Beauty Waltz (Tchaikovsky) • and more.

00145767 Book/Online Audio $10.99

RHAPSODY IN BLUE FOR PIANO DUET

George Gershwin
Arranged by Brent Edstrom
This intimate adaptation delivers access to advancing pianists and provides an exciting musical collaboration and adventure!

00125150 .... $12.99

CHART HITS FOR EASY DUET

10 great early intermediate pop duets! Play with a friend or with the online audio: All of Me • Grenade • Happy • Hello • Just Give Me a Reason • Roar • Shake It Off • Stay • Stay with Me • Thinking Out Loud.

00159796 Book/Online Audio $12.99

THE SOUND OF MUSIC

9 arrangements from the movie/musical, including: Do-Re-Mi • Edelweiss • Maria • My Favorite Things • So Long, Farewell • The Sound of Music • and more.

00290389..................... $14.99

RIVER FLOWS IN YOU AND OTHER SONGS ARRANGED FOR PIANO DUET

10 great songs arranged for 1 piano, 4 hands, including the title song and: All of Me (Piano Guys) • Bella's Lullaby • Beyond • Chariots of Fire • Dawn • Forrest Gump - Main Title (Feather Theme) • Primavera • Somewhere in Time • Watermark.

00141055 .... $12.99

STAR WARS

8 intergalactic arrangements of *Star Wars* themes for late intermediate to early advanced piano duet, including: Across the Stars • Cantina Band • Duel of the Fates • The Imperial March (Darth Vader's Theme) • Princess Leia's Theme • Star Wars (Main Theme) • The Throne Room (And End Title) • Yoda's Theme.

00119405..................... $14.99

HAL LEONARD PIANO DUET PLAY-ALONG SERIES

This great series comes with audio that features separate tracks for the Primo and Secondo parts – perfect for practice and performance! Visit www.halleonard.com for a complete list of titles in the series!

COLDPLAY

Clocks • Paradise • The Scientist • A Sky Full of Stars • Speed of Sound • Trouble • Viva La Vida • Yellow.
00141054..................... $14.99

FROZEN

Do You Want to Build a Snowman? • Fixer Upper • For the First Time in Forever • In Summer • Let It Go • Love Is an Open Door • Reindeer(s) Are Better Than People.
00128260..................... $14.99

JAZZ STANDARDS

All the Things You Are • Bewitched • Cheek to Cheek • Don't Get Around Much Anymore • Georgia on My Mind • In the Mood • It's Only a Paper Moon • Satin Doll • The Way You Look Tonight.
00290577..................... $14.99

HAL•LEONARD®
www.halleonard.com